SEATTLE

MADRONA PUBLISHERS, INC. • SEATTLE

DISCOVERED

BOB PETERSON

To LYNN COLBY PETERSON, who never ceases to amaze me

Copyright © 1976 by Madrona Publishers, Inc.
All rights reserved.
Printed in the United States of America

Library of Congress Cataloging in Publication Data

Peterson, Bob, 1941-
  Seattle discovered.

  1. Seattle—Description—Views. I. Title.
F899.S443P47   979.7'77   76-41333
ISBN 0-914842-13-7

Madrona Publishers, Inc.
113 Madrona Place East
Seattle, Washington 98112

Foreword

As the title says, Seattle is a city being discovered. This discovery is not the first one, for, stuck away in a remote corner of America, Seattle has been often forgotten and often rediscovered. In 1962, when a plucky overgrown town had the temerity to bid for national attention by staging a World's Fair, her discoverers found a pleasant city with many people leading "the good life" in a glorious natural setting. Now her discoverers are finding something more: that relative rarity in America, a city that is "making it," a place where one finds not another confirmation of the urban crisis, but a version of the urban promise. The glorious natural setting is still here, sailboats still bob at docks at the foot of lawns that stay green year-round, the signs of the good life still abound. But the good life is being harmonized with another concept, "city life." And that is the latest discovery: that Seattle is, in fact, a city — a citylike city.

First settled in 1851 as a distant outpost of westward migration, Seattle grew slowly but tenaciously until the turn of the century when there was a great rush of discovery and the population leaped ahead. That was the period in which the foundations were laid for making an unusually livable city: fine neighborhoods, democratically mixed and close-in; a lush system of parks and boulevards with views everywhere; solid traditions of clean government and good schools. Another boom during World War II stirred the city to new life and new confidence. But until a few years ago, what Seattle had that was most citylike was the host of problems facing all of America's cities: ethnic minorities being ghettoized; handsome older neighborhoods decaying as their residents fled to the suburbs; politicians dozing in caretaker roles; downtown merchants too dispirited to figure out how to reverse the trend towards stagnation.

Then about a dozen years ago, a lot of changes started to occur. Another great migration was altering Seattle, a new migration still going on (although slowed by the recession that struck Boeing in 1970) made up of professional people who could live and work in any city, of young people starting out their careers, of single people, highly-educated people, refugees from the outsized, wait-your-turn cities in the east and California. These latest explorers had come to discover how to have a city and a livable environment as well. America knows how to create huge cities, poor cities, rich cities, intense cities, maybe doomed cities. But in only a handful of places — Seattle chief among them — is she figuring out how to create cities in which one wants to spend one's whole life, raise one's children, and mix the challenge of a demanding career with the satisfactions of community and family life. In most American cities the good life is what one escapes to the suburbs to find. What has made Seattle the subject of so much national attention lately and has so exhilarated many of us here is our discovery that the good life can go along with city life.

I used to think, a few years ago, how uncitylike Seattle seemed. Pedestrians stood lamblike on the curbs waiting for the sign to tell them to "walk." (And *walk* they did: someone put a stopwatch on Seattle pedestrians and found that they actually did walk more slowly than people in other cities.) Drivers rarely honked — what kind of a city was this? Nightlife and downtown restaurants were spotty, sidewalk cafes were banned, wineshops were illegal. There was little ethnic variety. But then in the space of a very few years, remarkable transformations have taken place, aided by the grafting of the new migration onto Seattle's native energies. Government has been dramatically transformed and a new agenda has appeared: restore the old neighborhoods, dust off the city's historic districts, and expand her cultural and recreational amenities. A new entrepreneurial spirit has emerged, making the city's restaurants and shops almost as sophisticated and varied as those anywhere. The economy has broadened its range and remembered its international horizons. The downtown skyline seems to have jumped twenty stories in four years. And all of a sudden, after years of unrequited yearning for big league sports, we have four major league teams. A few months ago I was watching a football game in the Kingdome, sitting with 60,000 other people in that enormous room, and I realized how pleased we all were at how many of us there were and how loud was the sound of our voices. We were celebrating, not just our fledgling football team losing respectably, but the rediscovery of our common spirit as a city.

I find this spirit on almost every page of this book, in almost every one of Bob Peterson's pictures. Seattle, here, masses up like a *big* city. Her tall buildings form concentrations of interest so that the surrounding sea and mountains for once, photographically, do not overwhelm her. There is a lot to do and a lot of attractive people doing it. The frame is crowded and varied; the eye lingers a long time on each scene. People congregate with each other happily. The stride of a downtown shopper crossing Pine Street is that of a woman attacking Bloomingdale's. The faces are not reserved, not guarded, not fearful, not even enfolded in umbrellas as we often think of ourselves. No, these are bright, purposeful faces, unusually open and easy before the camera, their eyes fixed on a vivid outer world. There are a lot of people here one would like to get to know or have a drink with. This is not a city of strangers. It is a big, bustling city, charged with energy, but it is a congenial one. There is a rare urban spirit here.

To see Seattle this way is new and runs counter to our own cultural traditions. Our histories have until recently been the colorful sagas of gaudy sinners and waterfront brawlers, of radical politics and class warfare. We went along with looking at ourselves the way the rest of the country did, as just an extension of the romantic, colorful frontier: the Mercer girls, the gold rush, skid road and the general strike. We concocted, as Robert Cantwell writes in his book *The Hidden Northwest*, "the myth of a rip-roaring past of picturesque violence . . . a land of giants, a land of men to match mountains." What was overlooked was the real story — the forging of environmental politics and a habitable urban environment, of dour and dedicated visionaries who gave Seattle her lovely neighborhoods, her splendid parks and waterfronts, her hard-won and excellent public utilities, her internationally-oriented economy, and her progressive politics. They were city-builders, not frontiersmen, who in their day constructed Pioneer Square and the Pike Place Market. Until recently, however, these urban legacies had been allowed to decay while we romanticized the colorful characters who used to inhabit them or who wandered them like ghosts. Now the characters have faded and the places are being used as they were intended: business at the incomparable Market is better than it has been for forty years. Instead of being an Old-West frontier, Seattle is a new frontier, a model for others in how to save and enjoy cities. The fact is that history does not really count for much in Seattle. Bob Peterson does not show us architectural monuments moldering in tenement neighborhoods, or heroic statues looking down their bird-limed noses at their unworthy descendents. Chief Seattle on the cover shares the scene with an unawed, high-spirited little girl.

If we've been misled by our histories, our visual sense of the city has been misleading, too. For a generation of photographers — nature photographers, mostly — Seattle was a place to look away from. The city itself was a kind of embarrassment, hopelessly outclassed by the surrounding landscape. The view was across Lake Washington or Puget Sound, the entire composition framed in the foreground by a single bough from a city tree. Hilly Seattle was one gigantic look-out.

Not in this book. The breathtaking natural backdrop is still there, of course, but in Peterson's photographs it is "there" as it is in our daily lives. It pops up now and then when we are jogging, or riding the ferry, or cresting a hill in an unfamiliar neighborhood, or when the winter clouds suddenly abate. In this book it is the city itself that dominates, that presses into the forefront of our attention. No longer is Seattle like a Swiss mountain village, a negligible artifact in a vast landscape. Now it is a manmade creation of riveting interest. The powerful presences are not the mountains but the swooping freeway bridges, superferries bearing down on a shoreside fisherman, or the Domed Stadium. I admire particularly one picture of the sun setting, not over the Olympic Mountains, which are lost as usual in the clouds, but over the jagged, cantilevered form of Husky Stadium. A book about Seattle with this little of Mount Rainier cannot be all bad.

A final aspect of this discovery of Seattle — the city of Seattle, with its contemporary spirit — is her light. The quality of the light in Seattle is remarkable, particularly during those pervasively cloudy non-summer days when the gray northern light bathes the city in a soft, diffused, shadowless glow. It is a tempering light, one that modulates harsh contrasts and celebrates feathery monochromatic subtleties. It is a kind of light that is a trademark of Bob Peterson's photography, and for me, it is the visual key to understanding Seattle. This is a city without sharp contrasts of any sort, a city of muted clothes and manners, without excesses of wealth and poverty, where political divisions are shallow and social gradations are blurred. Life, like the light and the landscape, has soft edges.

This, I think, is the secret of Seattle now being discovered. Most American cities display harsh contrasts of wealth and poverty, sophistication and dreariness, flowers and iron. But these images of brutal extremes are missing in Seattle, where the reigning virtue (and sometimes the boring sin) is moderation. No city in America has a higher proportion of the middle class in its population. Her neighborhoods mix architectural styles and levels of income with the greatest of ease. Seattle is big, yet convenient; small, yet cosmopolitan; manmade and dense, yet everywhere edged and infiltrated by nature. What Seattle has, in short, is a human scale.

This "middleness' of Seattle makes her a difficult city to get into focus or appreciate. She lacks distinctiveness, style, regional flavor, or a dramatic history — she has been easy to feel modest and apologetic about. What one does see if one looks long and hard enough is a city in which one can live, one whose rhythms are agreeable to human needs. It is the realm, as Thomas Griffith recently wrote in the *Atlantic Monthly*, "of the decent middle." Not very exciting? Perhaps not — until we consider the alternatives.

DAVID BREWSTER

Acknowledgments

I could have been a great woodworker, but I came in two subscriptions short and the *Oakland Tribune* gave me a camera instead of the coveted jigsaw. So I took pictures.

I ought to thank Alice Peterson, my mother, because twenty-three years ago she said I wouldn't get any dinner until I picked out some photos, biked them to the post office, and mailed them to the Eastman Kodak high school photo contest. I didn't know we were having boiled broccoli that night. Later that year I won a $300 first prize for a photo of my sister, Anne, on a pony; and at twelve years old, I bought my first enlarger. Actually, I was really hooked on photography when I discovered that I could make my brother Jim's feet look enormous by placing them very close to the camera lens.

My dad, Pete the trainer, got me my first sideline photo passes, at the University of California, and by the time I was fifteen, I was the staff sports photographer for the *Berkeley Daily Gazette* — at ten dollars a week. My first big-time magazine job was for Peter Bunzel at *Seattle Magazine*, who kept me from going to New York too soon. In New York there were two good friends at *Life* who continually gave me good advice: Dave Scherman on living and working there, and Dick Pollard on when to leave.

I want to thank a few friends for invaluable help with this book: Lynn Peterson, who helped me, hid me, and protected me; Cole and Liza Peterson who played again and again in the same foregrounds until I got it right; Sam Angeloff, ex-*Time-Life* editor, who worked with both words and pictures; Stan Enfield and Ed Glazer at Glazer's Camera Store, who supported this project with patience and understanding; Hugh Stratford, the darkroom wizard who consistently saved my bacon; Dan Levant, who took almost all of the worrying off my shoulders; David Brewster, who was there at the beginning; Harold Kawaguchi, friend and confidant, who helped with editing, design, driving, and layouts, and was always available for Scotch and sushi when I needed him.

Finally, I couldn't have done the job without the steadying collaboration of my friend Julio Wilhelm, book designer and Catalonian gentleman, who spent many lost hours over the layout table with me.

BOB PETERSON

Downtown

From the north, and overhead   *(Following pages: First Avenue)*

Pioneer Square

Pioneer Square people

Traffic across Puget Sound

Pike Place Market

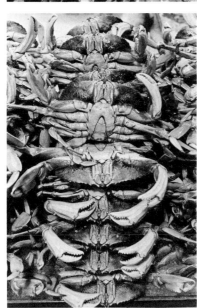

The Space Needle

Pacific Science Center

Wagner's Ring *at the Opera House*

*Backstage at Meany Hall: the University of Washington's
Philadelphia String Quartet*

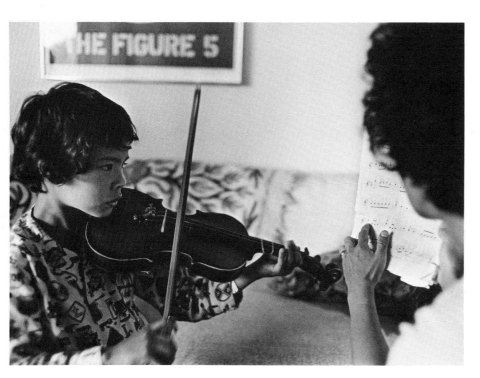

Centerstage at home: a second-year student violinist and his mother

Poncho's annual fund-raising auction for the arts

Seattle Youth Symphony

Conductor Vilem Sokol

Sculptor George Tsutakawa

Sculptor Jonn Geise

An opening at the Foster/White Gallery

First Chamber Dance Company

North toward Lake Union and Portage Bay

City houseboats

(Following page: the University of Washington)

The UW campus

Opening day of yacht season: past the UW and into Lake Washington

Water balloon welcome

Lake Washington Ship Canal and the Ballard Bridge

Shilshole Bay Marina

Salmon Bay Fishermen's Terminal

Government Locks

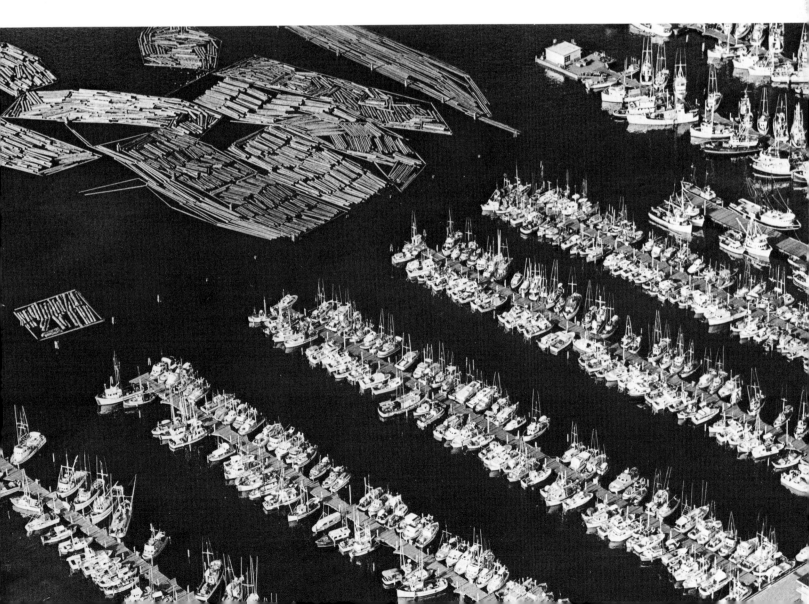

Fauntleroy ferry to Vashon Island

Duwamish Head in West Seattle

Making movies

The Kingdome

The Sounders

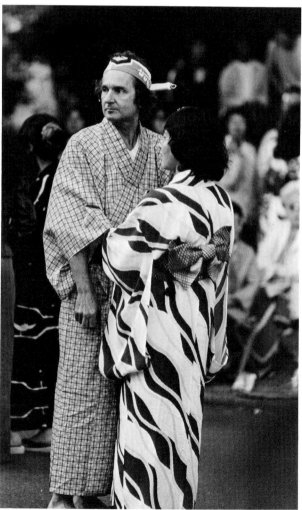

The Bon Odori festival

The International District's Hing Hay Park

Boeing Field

Gasworks Park

Sunday racing on Puget Sound

Seafair: Hydroplane racing on Lake Washington

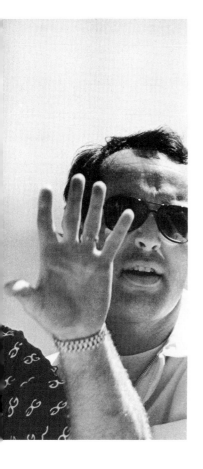

Evergreen Point floating bridge

The UW Crew on Union Bay

The University Arboretum

*The Seattle Marathon:
26 miles along Lake
Washington Boulevard*

Free theater: the Empty Space performs in Volunteer Park

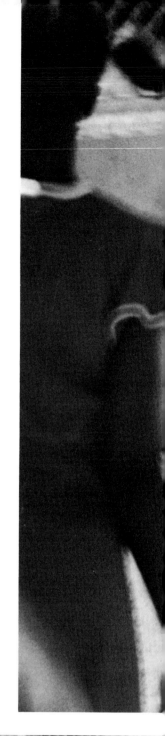

McGilvra School Playday

Woodland Park Zoo

(Following pages: across Lake Washington to Mercer Island and Mount Rainier)

Husky football at the UW Stadium

Seahawk football at the Kingdome

Supersonic basketball in the Coliseum

After 28 years as a night chef for Ivar, Mike Castillano retires: a Laigo/Castillano family party

(Following pages: Montlake Bridge)

People

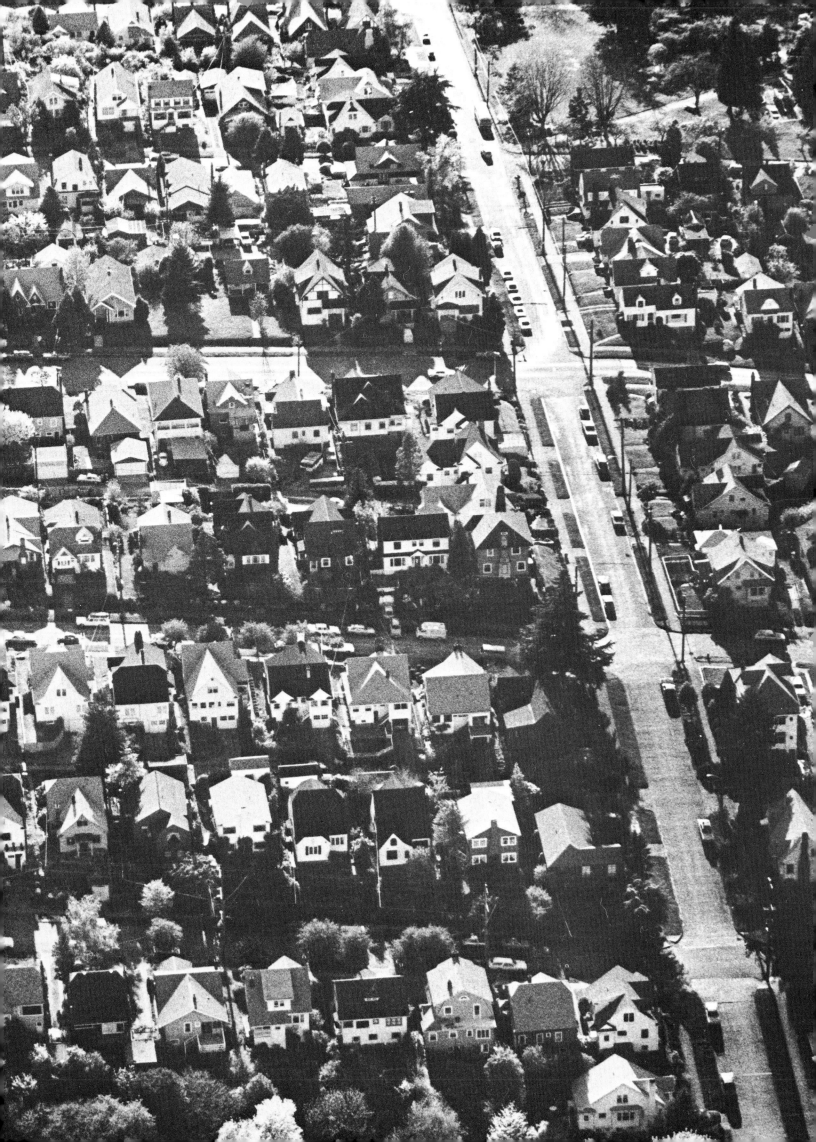